PENNY-WISE, FUN-FOOLISH

By Judy Delton

Pictures by Giulio Maestro

CROWN PUBLISHERS, INC., NEW YORK

10   9   8   7   6   5   4   3   2   1

The text of this book is set in 18 point Plantin. The illustrations are pre-separated
ink and pencil drawings prepared by the artist and printed in three colors.

Library of Congress Cataloging in Publication Data
Delton, Judy.
   Penny-wise, fun-foolish.
   Summary: An overly thrifty ostrich is taught
that sometimes spending money can be fun.
   [1. Jungle stories. 2. Animals—Fiction]
I. Maestro, Giulio. II. Title.
PZ7.D388Pe3   [E]   77-1582
ISBN 0-517-52996-3

TO JENNIFER ALICE DELTON

And all of the little animals

Who live under her bed

And inside her head

"Two hundred, three hundred, four hundred . . ." Ostrich counted out loud on her left wing feathers.

"My bank is nearly full," she said to herself. "I will be able to take a trip to America with Elephant."

Ostrich closed her bank and locked it.
She put it on the piano behind the
picture of Grandfather Ostrich.

Just then she saw Lizard at the
door with the *Jungle Journal*.
"Thank you," called Ostrich.
She picked up the newspaper.
She saw a coupon for a free photograph
at Parrot's Picture Palace.
She decided to cut it out.

As Ostrich got her scissors,

there was a knock on the door.

It was Elephant.

"I have just been to the new swimming

pool," he said. "It is a wonderful

place! There are six showers, and

a diving board that bounces!

Wait until you see it!"

Ostrich shook her head.

"Tsk tsk," she said. "I hear they charge money to get in. Why pay to swim when you can swim in the mudhole for free?"

"Some things are worth paying for," said Elephant.

"I don't know about that. Why just last night I watched a falling star. It was lovely. Just lovely. All for free. By the way, are you saving string for me? My ball is getting bigger and bigger."

Elephant sighed.

"Yes, Ostrich. I also have a gum wrapper
for your ball of tinfoil. I will give
it to you the next time I see you."

"Thank you," said Ostrich.

"Well, I must be on my way," said
Elephant. "Good-bye, Ostrich."

"Good-bye, Elephant."

Ostrich cut out the coupon for the free photograph. Then she saw several other coupons. She cut them out, too.

The next morning Ostrich woke up
early. She put on her dress and
her straw hat. She pinned an orchid
on her collar. Then she left for
Parrot's Picture Palace.
When she arrived, she gave
Parrot her coupon.
Parrot adjusted his glasses.
"FREE," he read, "TO ALL BLUE-EYED
OSTRICHES IN THE JUNGLE, ONE
PHOTOGRAPH IN LIVING COLOR."
"I have blue eyes," said Ostrich.
"So I see," said Parrot. "Step
right this way."

"Now, would you like to stand in front of a fig tree, or a pineapple plant?"
"A fig tree," said Ostrich.

Parrot fixed the camera.

Ostrich fixed her collar.

"When I say 'Cracker,' be sure
to smile," said Parrot.

"Okay," said Ostrich.

"Cracker," shouted Parrot.

Ostrich smiled, and Parrot snapped
the picture.

"It will be ready next week."

"Thank you," said Ostrich. "I will
    pick it up."

Then Ostrich went to Leopard's Store.
There was a long line.
"I hope all the teakettles are not
gone," thought Ostrich.
She tried to get through the door,

but Giraffe and Hippo were in the way.

"Excuse me," said Ostrich. "I have
a coupon for a free teakettle."

"So do we," said Giraffe. "Go to
the end of the line."

When Ostrich finally reached
the counter, she waved her coupon
. at Leopard.
Leopard gave her a blue
and white teakettle.
"Thank you very much," she said.

Then she took another coupon from her purse. It said: BUY TEN TYPEWRITER RIBBONS AT REGULAR PRICE, GET SIX MORE FREE. BABOON'S TYPE SHOP.

Ostrich hurried to Baboon's Type Shop.
"I would like to use this coupon,"
she said.
"You are very lucky," said Baboon.
"I have just sixteen typewriter
ribbons left."
Baboon wrapped the ribbons, and
Ostrich started for home.

She passed by Elephant's house.

He was taking out the garbage.

"Come in and get your string
and tinfoil," said Elephant.

"I believe I will," said Ostrich.

"I am tired from shopping."

She sat down on the sofa.

She put the string and gum
wrapper in her purse.

Then she told Elephant about the
photograph. She showed him the
teakettle and the typewriter ribbons.
Elephant laughed.
"But Ostrich, you don't have
a typewriter."

"That's true," said Ostrich. "But I have a coupon that says 'OPEN A SAVINGS ACCOUNT AT BOA-BANK AND GET A TYPEWRITER FREE.' I will put the money for our trip into the bank until we leave. That way I will get a free typewriter."

"I should have known," said Elephant.
"By the way, the carnival is coming here
  on Saturday. I hope we can go together."
"I'm afraid not," said Ostrich.
"I don't want to spend the money."
"I will be glad to pay your way,"
  said Elephant. "Please come. It will
  be more fun with a friend."

"No," said Ostrich. "If you want to waste money on yourself, that is one thing. But I cannot let you waste your money on me. I am saving my money for our big trip to America to see your brother in the zoo."

"You have *more* than enough money for
our trip," said Elephant. "All you do
is save. Save save save! Can't you
ever forget saving and have
a good time?"

"It never hurts to have something
for a rainy day," said Ostrich.

"I must go home now. I have a lot
to do. Thank you for the tinfoil
and the string."

"Stop in again," said Elephant sadly.

When Ostrich got home, she put the
teakettle on the stove and the typewriter
ribbons in a drawer. She wound the
string onto her big ball of string. She
rolled the tinfoil onto her big ball of
foil. Then she pasted green stamps
in her stamp book.

"Another full book!" she said.

Then she took a nap.

She slept for several hours.

When she got up, she made a cup of

tea in her new teakettle.

Then she sat down to read the

evening newspaper.

"Elephant Olympics over!" it said
on the front page.
"Ostriches molt early this year,"
it said on the second page.
When Ostrich turned to the third page,
a piece of paper fell to the floor.
Ostrich picked it up. It said:
FREE WITH THIS COUPON. ONE ADMISSION
TO THE JUNGLE CARNIVAL FOR ALL
LEFT-WINGED OSTRICHES WITH ONE TAIL
FEATHER MISSING. ALSO GOOD FOR FREE
RIDES AND FREE BANANA SODAS.
Ostrich ran to the mirror.
"For goodness sakes," she said. "I am
a left-winged ostrich! And one of my
tail feathers is missing!"

She ran to the telephone.

"Elephant!" she shouted. "I can go to the carnival for free! There is a coupon in my newspaper for all left-winged ostriches with one tail feather missing! Elephant, that's me! Isn't it wonderful? Now we can go together!"

"I'm glad," said Elephant. "I will meet you at Coconut Corner at nine-thirty tomorrow morning. I will bring a bag of peanuts."

"Good," said Ostrich. "And I will bring olive and cucumber sandwiches!"

The next morning Ostrich made
the sandwiches and put them in her
picnic basket. She sang as she walked
down the path to Coconut Corner.
Elephant waved when he saw her.
"You are right on time!" he said.
"Yes," said Ostrich. "I am so excited.
I have never been to a carnival. They
always charge admission, you know."
Elephant did not say anything.

As they walked along, they talked
about the fun they would have.
Before long, they could see the
carnival gate ahead.

When they reached the gate, Elephant
paid Zebra the entrance fee. He also
bought a book of tickets for rides
and soda pop.

Then Ostrich gave Zebra her coupon.
Zebra gave her a book of tickets.
"Go right in," he said. "You can use
the tickets for anything you want."

Elephant and Ostrich walked toward
the rides.

"What shall we try first?" asked Elephant.

"The ferris wheel," said Ostrich.

Ostrich and Elephant got on the ferris wheel. Ostrich covered her eyes when they got to the top. Elephant looked down and waved. The ferris wheel went around six times. Then it stopped. Elephant and Ostrich got off.

"That was scary!" said Ostrich.

"But I liked it!"

"Let's ride it again," said Elephant. They took three more rides on the ferris wheel.

Then they rode on the merry-go-round.

After that they went for a ride in

the rocket.

Ostrich straightened her sunbonnet

as they got off.

"That was fun," she said.

"Yes, it was," said Elephant. "Now

I'm hungry."

They spread their tablecloth on the grass under a shady tree. They ate sandwiches, and drank banana sodas through straws.

After lunch they took turns pitching
balls for prizes. Ostrich won a big
stuffed chimpanzee.

Then they watched a puppet show.
When it grew dark, they started
for home.

"My oh my!" chattered Ostrich.

"I have never had such a good time."

"I'm glad," said Elephant.

"But I'm sorry you had to pay," said
Ostrich. "Too bad there wasn't a
coupon for elephants with one
toenail missing. That would
have been nice."

Elephant looked embarrassed.

"Er—Ostrich—there is something I—
er—should tell you. Ah—I put that
coupon in your newspaper. I paid Zebra
for your tickets ahead of time."

Ostrich stopped walking.

"You *paid!*" she said.

"Yes," said Elephant. "But didn't
you have a good time?"

"Why yes, of course. I can't remember
when I had more fun! But you paid.
You paid for both of us!"

"Sometimes spending money is worthwhile," said Elephant.

Ostrich thought awhile.

Then she said, "What are you doing next Saturday?"

"Nothing," said Elephant. "Why do you ask?"

"Well—ah—I would like to try that new swimming pool. I have always wanted to take a shower. And I could wade far deeper in a swimming pool than I can in the mudhole."

"Fine!" said Elephant. "We will
go together!"
"And," said Ostrich, "I will pay."
Elephant laughed.
"And I will let you."